A Sticky Problem

Karen J. Guralnick
Illustrated by Kathryn Mitter

Harcourt Achieve

Rigby • Saxon • Steck-Vaughn

www.HarcourtAchieve.com
1.800.531.5015

"Patches," said Eric, "catch the ball!"

Eric's dog had been really good at
catching balls this week.
He could always catch the ball.

CRASH!
The ball hit Mom's lamp.

"Oh no!" said Eric.
"If Mom finds out I broke her lamp,
I'll be in trouble!
Maybe I should use Mighty Glue.
I've seen Mom use it to fix lots
of things."

Eric ran to get the Mighty Glue and
took the broken lamp to his bedroom.

He picked up two pieces and
quickly glued them together.
As he tried to pick up the next piece,
he realized that his thumb and finger
were stuck together.
When he couldn't pull his fingers apart,
he decided to try to wash off the glue.
"If this doesn't work, I don't know what
I'll do," Eric said.

While he was washing his hands,
Eric heard his mom come into
the house.

"Eric," said Mom, "it's time
for dinner.
Ask Gina to go to the kitchen.
I'll change my clothes, and then we
can start cooking."

"Okay!" said Eric.

Washing his hand didn't get
the glue off.

Eric decided to hide his hand
until he could think of another way
to unstick his fingers.

He told Gina to go to the kitchen
to help Mom.
Then he ran to the kitchen to put
on an oven mitt.

When Gina saw Eric, she asked, "Why are you wearing an oven mitt?"

Eric smiled and said, "I'm wearing it because I'm ready to cook."

Gina said, "You don't need that yet." When she pulled off the oven mitt, some fuzzy pieces came off and stuck to Eric's hand.

"I need to wash this off," said Eric, running to the bathroom.

After he pulled off most of the fuzz,
he asked Patches, "Lotion will take the
glue off my hand, won't it?"

"*Woof*," said Patches.

While Eric was opening a bottle
of Gina's lotion, it spilled all over him.

He was about to clean it up
when Gina called through the door.
"What are you doing?
Dinner is almost done,
and you didn't help."

"I'll be out soon," he said.
He quickly washed off the lotion and
opened the door.

"Why are you wet," Gina asked,
"and why do you smell like flowers?"

"I spilled your lotion," he said.

Gina ran to the kitchen and said,
"Mom, Eric spilled my lotion!"

Mom said that Eric would need to buy
new lotion for Gina.

Mom called Eric to the table.
When he got to the table, he just stared at his soup.

Mom asked, "Why aren't you eating?"

Eric held up his hand.

"What happened?" Mom asked.

Eric told Mom about the broken lamp.

Mom wasn't happy, but she got
some Glue-Off.
She showed Eric how to use it.

"Thanks, Mom," Eric said.
"I'm really sorry that I broke
your lamp."
Then he smelled his shirt and said,
"And I'm *really* sorry that I used
Gina's lotion."